lemon

lemondrops

DWES

This is for all those who read my poetry and felt something within it. I am forever in debt to your support and understanding.

This is for myself and being able to find a way to heal in more ways than one.

Contents

SWEET

A note to all who sat beside me, smiling, while everything began to go down smooth.

I wait for the day
When we look out
And see the field of flowers
Wrapped in plaid blankets
With sharp cups of tea
In a land unknown
The only path needed
Is clasped hands
You next to me

Your trace
Became my backbone
Your fingers
Created strength
And showed me
That I can
Stand

(deoxyribose)

Home:

When I thought
Of it was
Two walls

You sat
Next to me

Two lips

The memory of
Your hands
On my body

The only stability
I need

(you came running to hold my hand again)

I closed my eyes
To sleep
I thought of you

I knew
If I opened them now
In the dead of night

I would never sleep:

The dark would show
No outline of your body

I would know you were
Out there somewhere
Wishing for me

I knew
A star would die
From your wish

Because
I was yours
Even now

(sleep walking)

The light streaking
Through the sky
Clasping hands
Was the only
Way I could

See

The shadows of
Your back
The clean bare

Curves

Of the person
Who would
Never want
To stop loving

Me

Together
We circled
Each other
Never to
Let go

(the sky broke open only for us)

Our bed had begun to smell
Of an aromic musk
Of bodies entwined
Dreaming

For you
The hush of your secrets
Would have been more distracting
Then bare legs in your sheets
Your eyes looking at me
Only me
I would be blinded
By the knowing of you, just
Wanting me
Touching me
I would have shuddered;
Memory and longing
May be all that I can leave
In this world

(stardust)

Just lay on me
On our tattered
Couch
Make me
Feel that the only
Pressure of the world

        Your body on mine
        Is what I could
        Forever live with

Touch me: please
When you touch me
Flames don't consume me
Clouds come over me
Take me away
To the place
I wish never to leave

One day
I will stop missing you
No longer needing
Your hands on me
Instead your arms around me
Laying side by side
No longer in a grass bed
Now we sleep in clings of sheets
Our heads on pillows
Covering one another
Our heat all we need
Snow covered streets
No worrying tonight

Is this how life
Will remain

The median
Of calm
Alert
Of never letting
Go
Only knowing

The beauty of winter
Into
Spring

Smell and soft wind
Being aware of what once was
The bitter sting
Soft drops
Of new snowflakes
On upturned
Faces

In the grove
I walked
And let the smell
Take over
The feeling of
Being surrounded
Overwhelming, me
I bowed to those trees
The warm flesh
Seeping into my skin
As the smell consumed me
Rubbing me raw
Making me fresh
(Sweet)
The remainder of the day

I could only hope
That the wind
I felt on my fingers
Kiss my lips
Once again
Only to undo
The memory of you

Once we look
In each others eyes
Again
There would be no past
Only now

...

Placed in tight skin
The world no longer
Touches you
Not even the anger
Hurt
The acceptance
Of all that lays around you
Becomes the air
You breathe
You decided to let it all slide in
Touch you
Never let it change you

Early morning
With the new light
Brings the memories
Of the bad
Removes them
With all the pride and love
Held in the voice that held your hand
For many years
Even if for support most
Times
It was always there
Even in pain
There was always pride
And doesn't that count

For anything?

Surrounding
Around me
The life I live

Life meant living
Jump of faith

Discovery of self
In words
The steam
And smell of the coffee
I've drunk
So many times
So many cups
Sitting here

Sometimes

I decide
That I was important
That I am
The one longed for
The words I said
My smile imprinted
In the back of your mind
The petals pressed

Reminding

You that my hand
Meant something
And those looks
Were not just for me
But for you
For once
This one time
I am missed
The aroma
Once smelled again
I couldn't help but
Smile

Make me your concert
A solo song
To shake my ribs

Restart my heart
Make it yours again
With the echo

Of each song

Again
More
Encore

Behind my eyes
Only I could feel
The relief of knowing

Happiness
Was not what everyone felt
But,
Sat with only some
Shared the bench with few

I was one

That just kept watching
In the park
Saw only seats taken
Never empty
Never waiting

I keep confusing
All that I
Have fought for
For all that
I do not have

The day will come
When forgiveness
Is more than just
The need to forget
But the want
To once again
Be together

Tears dripped
Out
Through every pore
Arms
Squeezing
Myself
Cleansing
Pushing

All the impurities

All the build up

I knew
Once I dried
Sat in the sun
Skin tightening
I would be better
I would see myself again

And know

I made
Myself whole

I wait
Wait
Even though I know
I don't need to stand
By the ticking
Time clock
Hiding in the shadows
It's easier to be in the
Dark
The step in the light
Knowing it might burn

Know that when all eyes
See me they may shrink away
And wish me into the dark
I know though
That I am light
When they see
They won't shriek
But come closer
And feel the depth
Warmth that radiates
And know they will
Stand by me and accept
All the cracks of cold that
Seep through
Gravitating more towards
Warmth and laughs
Me

Instead of praying
I sat and waited
For the silence
To never answer

My heart to stop beating
My breath to slow
Reminding me
That all is well
I can live again

I wait
Sit
Hoping something
Comes
That will tell
Me
The world is calm
Finally calm
And I can breathe
Easy again

This time I welcome it
The fever
That built up
Would no longer
Be infection

Instead of screaming
Flames
The hush of
A winter storm would
Take place

I could feel my heart
Stop pounding
I could think again

Alone
A welcome
Turn of events

I blew
Smoke
Billowing before me
Was that of my past

Inhaling the cool air
My lungs filled
With the present
Crystallizing: despair left behind

Letting all new
Sit and lay
Blooming into glistening flowers

Cracking when I laughed
Dust gliding through my bloodstream
Surrounding all anger and fear
Dissipating into calm

In sadness I rose
Between the gasps
Of air
I found my own breath
Between the tears
Pressing
Down my face
I found myself cleansing
The hardwood
Floor
I screamed
Only to finally find my voice

Even though
You are my better half
I no longer lean
On your strength
I lean on you for
Only sanity
Within the insanity
I became strong again

SOUR

A note to all who sat beside me and
felt the bitter aftertaste of my touch.

The tale is this
That it was only a tale
Of love from one side
Each taking its own turn
Too late to ever be together

One day broken
The other all regret
One day filled with fire
The other tears
Made the flowers
Bloom

The secret being
The world would have to
Crack in
Two
For the light of one day
The dark of the other
Mix together

Isn't that how the stars
Were
Created

To show the light in the dark

One day; light making you wish so hard
The other; shows you the depths of the dreams you always had

They call her
Wild thing
Because
She

             Startled

At the touch
Of all those

             Human hands

It came
In bitten nails
Clothes heaping
The floor
The exhaustion after
(1)2 hours sleep

I don't know
But I know it's gone
The way a building crumbles
And you only notice
When it's not there
No standing skeleton
Only the dirt
Being moved
While driving by

One day
My heart will stop
Beating because
The expected pounding
Will be too great
The need for life
Too much for one organ
The dependence
Will push it to explode
To give up
Realization
That one day it all ends
Why not today
Why not now
When soon
In months
Years
Decades away
Why
Not
Now

I began to jump
At my own
Shadow
When
I learned that
Others could step on it

I began to fear myself
When I learned no one
Else would fear me

My words became air

Easily sucked
In
Taken from my own
Lips

I would bloom

No one watered me
I cried to grow

In the darkness I sat
Shrinking away from the sun
Finding home there
The only place where
          Belong
Was an unrecognizable light

Your eyes
A mirth
Expansive as the sea
Meeting the sky
Lost sensations
Of an astronaut
Drifting with the stars
The weightless reality
Of where you are
The difference being
Lost sensation
Never leaving
Always wondering

Is there more out there

The decision
That the world
Took something
From you
That I
Was not enough
No good trade- no lasting replacement
Giving you nothing back

The sky opened
Up and took
From you
Closing up after

Only I still standing
There
Beside you

My hand dissolving in your palm
You saw the stars
Wishing hard enough
To become infinity
In the darkness that surrounded

Infinity no longer
Meant me
Only the possibility
Of everything
You could
Be

My back turned
I wish upon
Those stars that night
Above us
That you see
More should have been said
That grasped hands were
Never fate
Only fatal

The stinging reminder
That the only love lingering
Was between your legs

The only love in site-
Stains of red
From glasses
Of cranberry juice

Maybe I avoid water
Because if I jump
I may never come back
The stones in the pit of my stomach
Weighing me down

My tears made a pool at my feet
Those walking by
Walked around
Never falling in
Instead covering it with a jacket
In hopes it would no longer exist
Just saying hi
Continuing on

To see if I could walk through sadness too
I stepped forward
Falling deep
Knowing in an instant
They. Kept. Walking.

I cried because
You never left
You waited
Until someone
Could no longer
Take
Standing on
Broken glass
The knock out
Through toxins

Then you
Screamed
Yelled
Asking
How could
I ever

Leave

Each stair creaked
An expectation
To fall through

Puncture a lung
Ribs wrapping around me
Surrounding me
To never ending darkness
Of the deepest basement

But then
Grasping in air
I pulled
Lights illuminate
I am fine
Darkness inevitable
The next day
Unavoidable

Strength came
When you pushed
Me down through the clouds

    Reminding me

That when I fell
I would not be caught

My spine cracking
Against the pavement
Shards of bone
Piercing my heart

Picking
Piece by piece
Laying before me

    Fractions of myself

I saw in-front of me
Startling realization
That only I could
Recreate myself

Maybe I'll be

Like the
Last think you ate
Dropping to your stomach
Weighing you down

For the rest of the day

Reminding you
That you should never
Eat
Something so sour
In the mornings

I turned away
Your ashes caught me
Brushed my cheek
Pose petals forming
A slap in the face
Kissing too hard
For so long
That's all you would
Take-accept
From me
In the end
All you wanted
Was a swollen face
Of goodbyes

Your whispers made me shudder
It became a creaking house
Forming all the ghosts
Forgotten souls
To come up
Grab my hands
Claw my throat

Dragging me down into the nightmares
I always believed would have left me by now

Then you whispered
And everything shrieked
I knew not to scream

But to run
      run
          run

Once my back was turned
Once you no longer saw my eyes
You could not blow ash into my face

No longer blinding me
Collecting in my lungs
I ran
      ran
          ran

Into the sea
There I sailed free
         free
            free

Hush
Quiet
Please
Ncvcr quict
Even in the middle
Of night

Dead of night

Just one moment
Of quiet
Hush
Please

How do I
Ask for forgiveness
When I didn't care
About sorry
Sorry being turned
Around (x3)
Grasping
Hoping for a better tomorrow

You were a bad aftertaste
Only memories
The night was bitter
That taste in your mouth
A lingering bite
Of trying to remember
If there was anyone else
Trying to forget your lips

You lit the candle
So the burning
Wouldn't just be inside
Your heart
Engulfing you
The smoke you choked
And garbled
Wouldn't be from
The burn you couldn't escape
But the comfort you desired
From the outside source
Of self-choice
Seeing the flames
That became so familiar

(youwalkedintotheflames)

The stars
Refused to be covered
By clouds
Sky empty
The memory lasting
Longer than your
Lips against my skin
Why am I left
With the memory
Of never ending

....

Why do you get my mind
When all I get is
A sigh of your
Breath leaving
The question
Of infinity
Boxing me in

Held hands
Are meant
To be let go

(airplanesflying)

When you were gone:
Shadows followed me
Clouded my every
Breath
          Stealing   clutching   grabbing
Breathing it in
Reminding me
What would happen
If it ever left

Shadows

Ever leaving
Never returning
The breath
It took
The heart beats
Collected
Grasped from my chest

I am not a song that you turn on and off when you're not in the mood

While you were gone
I found

Inevitable

Felt the darkness

Even in the sun
I grasped at the chance
Of the shadow never next to me
Never controlling
When you look at me
Everything it took
Would be restored
By your
       Touch
       Breath
I would be me again

I wait
Knowing. the memory
Will. evade you
One. sullen night
Twisted. with dreams
Your. sheets
Soaked
My. tears coasting every inch
The. dreams begin to invade us both
Neither. close by
Only. the dreams
The. memories
Of. the nights
Forgotten

I do fucking wander
Because
I am fucking lost

(travelersanxiety)

About the Author
Why I Wrote This

Devon Ward is a poet and student based in Buffalo, New York. This is her first collection of poetry where she hopes that someone out there can find some sort of comfort in the words. That the heart may drop and it's because you realize you're not alone.
When she is not writing she is with her fiancé and her dog, Baxter. As well as, constantly reading and hoping she becomes a nurse.

81209236R00040

Made in the USA
Middletown, DE
21 July 2018